MW01536963

FINDING COURAGE
IN THE CONFLICT

Mirlo Liendo

Copyright © 2021 by MirloLiendo

All rights reserved. No part of this book may be reproduced or used in any manner without written permission of the copyright owner except for the use of quotations in a book review. For more information, address: mirloliendo@gmail.com

FIRST EDITION

ISBN: 978-1-7777962-1-1 Paperback

www.mirloliendo.com

Table of Contents

〜

You deserve so much more than *struggle love.*

Healthy love exists. Please do not let this world fool you into thinking you need abuse, humiliation, or to be someone else's saviour to earn the love and respect you want for yourself.

The narcissist is not someone who is broken, to be fixed. They are not your problem. They will not change.

This is who they are as abusers. This is their personality, and this is how they will continue to navigate the world with or without you.

A Letter from the Author

~

Before we begin, here are some housekeeping suggestions for you, the reader:

1. This is an outline of what the abuse looks like in its most subtle and often confusing ways. This is not every day. There are more good days than abusive ones, especially in the beginning when you are being love bombed and your boundaries are being tested. Over time, the line will continue to be crossed, meaning that subtler one-offs will become *normal*. The line continues to be pushed until you don't recognize your life. It's like a dripping faucet. It doesn't seem like a big deal until you get an astronomical water bill and your sink is corroded – by then, the damage is already done.

2. If you live in what you believe to be an abusive relationship, I highly suggest that you keep this book outside of your home. If he is going through your belongings – and he/she likely is – he/she *will* find this book. This does not need to be one more thing to draw the potential of violence or verbal assault to yourself.

Leave it at work, at a friend's house, or with a trusted family member. Just do not bring it home.

In addition, the examples included are a reflection of my story. Narcissists are not just intimate partners; they are parents, siblings, neighbours, coworkers and bosses.

The purpose of this book began as an outlet to help me heal. Instead, it has turned into a form of communication to share the signs with those who are secretly surviving very similar experiences. Now, the purpose is to have the same conversation with you that I wished someone had with me all those years ago. I want you to catch the signs early and make a more informed decision on how you will proceed in every relationship you participate in.

I would like to start by sharing with you something that I found profoundly moving when I was in the eye of the storm. Years before I had moved out and moved on, I had a moment of clarity. Well, as much clarity that can be declared when you have been completely depleted. It's that with swollen eyes, empty tear ducts, broken capillaries on my face, and finger marks bruised into my neck – I couldn't love someone enough to make them stop hurting me.

I promise you, *I have tried.*

Being in an abusive/narcissistic relationship will have you feeling like you are on top of the world at the start; once they have you where they want you, they will have you feeling confused and worthless more than anything else.

It will start with you not wanting to leave because they need you, and it will end with you not leaving because you believe you need them. If you have ever questioned your own ability to judge whether your relationship is healthy, I hope this book can provide you with some clarity.

Just for reference, I am and always have been what society considers a strong and independent woman. I am outspoken, confident, funny, charismatic, and warm. Not a single person in my life would have imagined I would be an eighteen-year survivor of intimate partner violence.

I say this only to put things in perspective.

Society will have us believing that abuse survivors are weak or willing participants in our own demise. We do not lack the intelligence or strength to recognize and leave these relationships; we simply have not developed the boundaries to identify the line in the sand – the *non-negotiables*.

I had spent nearly two decades desperately trying to change who I was, what I did, what I thought, and how much I loved – so he would feel loved by me. I wanted nothing more than to be able to pour my love into him so he could feel safe, understood, and appreciated. Ultimately, I wanted him to choose me as his person.

It wasn't until I was flat-out desperate for safety as a woman and a mother that I saw how much he really hated me, even through his own fake tears. I fully understood the magnitude of what my life had become.

Although I understand that there are immeasurable lessons in this journey, I still wish someone had told me years earlier that my love was not enough and that I needed to save my children and myself.

I would also like to add, not every narcissist is violent, but every narcissist is an abuser. In my case, verbal and physical violence was how my ex chose to control me and force me into submission. This violence does not occur in every case. For some, it is a cycle of cheating and manipulatively making you believe you are responsible for their behaviour. For others, it's a game of making you chase them for crumbs of attention or affection. Abuse is abuse. The roots of emotional abuse can be just as devastating as the roots of physical abuse, and a narcissist will always emotionally abuse and manipulate you.

You will find in between chapters, there is a space for reflection. I encourage you to dig deep and honestly document your feelings when you have finished the chapter. These documented entries will help you maintain a clear record of patterns and how they have made you feel, especially when they return to the cycle of love-bombing and re-writing history. It is for you to remember who you are dealing with at their core when their gaslighting causes you to question your reality. They will serve as a reminder of the insidious nature of your relationship and will hopefully allow you to gain the courage to leave.

My only hope is that you are given something you can relate to, a story that allows you to realize that you are not alone – one that will allow you to find your courage in the conflict and the courage to leave.

I also want to preface this information because I am not a doctor, nor am I entering this space with degrees in psychology. I have worked in the world of social work for decades, but I am not coming to you from this place. I firmly believe that sharing our human experiences will allow us to believe what we are really seeing in our partners. It is not our wounds that unite us. It is our healing.

What I *am* an expert in is my life. I am an expert in falling deeply in love with a man who hated me because he hated himself. I am an expert in how to leave someone after eighteen years of my life, with my children, and very little else. I have spent a decade reading and researching narcissistic personality disorder on my own. I have spent years attending trauma therapy in an attempt to understand how I could have fallen victim to abuse and, more importantly, how to never find myself in this hell again.

I am not only an expert in surviving, but I am an expert in thriving.

Like many of you, there was a time I felt like a complete fool for "allowing" myself to have been manipulated and abused by the man I loved. I felt stupid, unworthy, confused, and like I was a huge failure. I made mistakes in the process of leaving, some of which have cost me the safety of my children, a lot of time, and more money than I would care to admit.

However, the bottom line is this – I, like you, was carefully chosen. These abusers seek and attach themselves only to those who make them look good. It is our big hearts, our loyalty, and our compassion for people that led them to us. It was their manipulation and deceit that caused the abuse.

We are not to blame for any part of this process. Not the time you have spent in the situation, not the times you may have left him/her and returned, not for being oblivious to the signs, and in no way – for not leaving him at the first sign of trouble.

It is hard to believe that someone can want you in his or her, life and not like you. That someone can lay with you while resenting the ground you walk on. That someone can reap the benefits of your participation in their life and hate you at the same time – but here we are.

The truth is we are incredible people. We are interesting, intelligent, strong, and capable. We are loving, sincere, and honest. We are everything they are not.

When I left my ex-husband I was a shell of who I once was. I will never be the same person I was before we met. It has taken years of therapy, counselling, fighting the judicial system, blood, sweat, tears, doubt, amazing friendships, and equally as incredible mentors to get to this point; but I am proud of the woman I have become.

To the women in my life who have held me up, wiped my tears, brushed off my shoulders, and reminded me of who I am

– there are no words to express my gratitude. They created a safety net for me when I needed them the most, and I am hoping this is what I have to offer you. Some hope, and a reminder of who you are, and more importantly, who you are not.

The following fourteen chapters will outline red flags or warning signs that I saw but was not aware of as signs of pending abuse.

Find Your Courage in the Conflict

~

Ultimately, what matters most is not the label or a diagnosis. It is not about fancy academic language or research materials. It's that you can identify abusive behaviours and patterns. I hope you can read this and take away some courage to learn and understand what abuse looks like.

It is about identifying:

How you are being treated.

What the abuser says and does that is hurtful to you and your relationship.

What it feels like to be unheard.

That humiliation is not a joke, and your feelings should never be dismissed.

What abuse looks and sounds like when you are dealing with a master manipulator.

How they react when you set a boundary or say *no*.

What being emotionally and physically safe looks and feels like.

It is less about why you are being abused and more about it not being your fault. By the end of this book, I want you to know that you are not responsible for how others act. You are only responsible for what you do next.

CHAPTER 1:

❧

Mr. Charming

Not every charming person is a narcissist, but every narcissist is charming. You know that person who can walk into a room and take up all the space? The party starter. The leader. The loudmouth. The one who needs to take centre stage. The one with the most charm and charisma. The one who makes you feel like you are the most important person in the world.

Alternatively, the charm is not always loud and proud. People who ooze charm can be equally as discreet, quiet, shy, and even nerdy – but there is that "something" that makes them stand out.

This is who I am referring to.

For the purposes of this book, we will call my ex "Richard."

We were in high school when Richard and I met. I had just taken a year and a half off because I had a baby, and I had attended this particular high school because it had a childcare centre where I could leave my son while I completed my diploma. Richard was eighteen, and I was nineteen – this is our not-love story.

This high school was a new school to me, and I didn't know anyone there. I was single, raising my son alone, and had spent years being told that I was destined to be a single mother for as long as I lived because I had "another man's" baby. It's safe to say I wasn't even considering a relationship at the time because I genuinely felt unworthy. I didn't have the time or the desire to be rejected by someone I had feelings for.

However, the second semester came around. I was in my first period World Issues class when Richard walked in late, loud, and with what appeared to be all the confidence in the world. He was taller than everyone else in the class, but more than just his height, he had a gorgeous smile, and he walked in as if he owned the classroom. A group of young men looked happy to see him and welcomed him with your typical teenage boy rowdiness. The look on our teacher's face, however, was what sealed the deal for me. Our alpha male teacher looked intimidated and irritated. I was at a loss for words and completely intrigued.

He would catch me watching him, or I would see him watching me – this was something that was always up for debate even until the day I left him. The bottom line was, we were constantly watching each other. It was not long before we spent time outside of school together, talking for hours, comparing music, and watching movies. He liked all of the same films I did, listened to the same music, and would share similar views on life. Richard was more attentive than anyone else in my life, and he was such a great listener. When I talked about things I loved, he would smile and agree with me, encouraging me to stay on course because I had the tenacity to do anything I set my mind to. He believed in me when no one else did.

Or so I thought.

Richard felt too good to be true. He would tell me that he had never known anyone like me, who shared many of the same interests and thoughts about the world as he did. I ate it up – all of it. He would laugh at my jokes and tell me how he admired me for being such an attentive mother to my son. We began spending more time together, and when he started spending time with my two-year-old, my heart would melt just watching them play. My son was the key to my heart, and once he knew this, Richard became my son's biggest fan.

Here we were. I had somehow found a man who loved my son and me despite my community labelling me a failure.

It gets better, though. As the years went on, I became even more drawn to his charm. Not just with me, but with everyone, everywhere we went. If he wasn't shovelling the neighbour's driveway after a snowstorm so they could park with ease when they arrived home, he was helping a cousin paint their house. Richard was good with children and was like the Pied Piper. He was the game starter, the fun uncle. He was the first to run to a stranger's aid if their car broke down or they needed help unloading groceries into their car. He was the first to jump out of his seat and grab a broom if something spilled or broke while at someone else's house.

He was everyone's first choice for a godparent, groomsman, or best man, and he was an uncle to everyone's child.

Richard was an incredible man in the eyes of the community. It wasn't long though before he began subtly tearing me down and taking back all of those empowering things he had once said to me. He was devaluing me.

You see, they use their charm as collateral when it's time to start abusing you. Narcissists create this larger-than-life persona, so you feel lucky to have them. The intention is for others to question your sanity or judgement if you consider leaving. They make being around them feel so good; you cannot imagine not having access to them.

In my own experience, the devaluing began once I became pregnant with Richard's baby. This was unplanned, but how this experience was dismissed by him was definitely a precursor to how the remainder of our relationship would unfold.

I was entering my first year of college. I did a pharmacy-bought pregnancy test without telling him because I didn't want to scare him unnecessarily, and it was positive. Here I was, twenty-one years old and looking at my four-year-old son with a racing heart, sweaty palms, and honestly – some excitement that my little guy was going to have a brother or sister.

I picked up the phone with what felt like cotton balls in my throat. It was a Saturday afternoon, and I hadn't heard from him in a few days. I must have dialed his number a hundred times and hung up when I got to the last digit. This was not like me; I was direct, almost too blunt sometimes. I was never afraid of confrontation, and I wasn't afraid to communicate my thoughts or feelings with anyone. But this time, I was scared.

When I built up the nerve to use my shaking fingers to dial the last number, he answered.

"Hello"

"Hi, uhhhh...we need to talk, can you come over for a bit?"

"I was just there a few days ago. I'm busy, I'll call you tomorrow." I could hear his brothers and his cousin laughing and playing music in the background before he hung up the phone.

What?! Is he for real? This was the first time in over a year I had ever made a request of him, and he's too busy to come over for a few minutes? I thought.

So I did what many twenty-one-year-olds would do when they felt like they were in crisis. I called back.

"What do you want? I'm trying to get ready to go out," Richard spat.

"I said I needed to speak with you for a few minutes, I never ask you for anything..." I responded.

All I heard was a click and dial tone.

You know when you are so angry you can hear and feel your blood pulsing through your ears? I couldn't catch my breath. I didn't even know what to do or how to feel. So I called back.

He picked up the phone and barked, "Stop calling me! I said I'm fucking busy!"

Before he hung up on me again, I could still hear his brothers and cousin in the background. They were listening to all of this.

He had *never* spoken to me like this before. I was so hurt. With tears streaming down my face, what felt like rocks in my throat, and a heart being crushed in my chest – I called back. This time, I said what I needed to say before he could yell at me and hang up.

Richard picked up the phone, and I said, *"I'm pregnant."* That was it. At that point, I just wanted him to know, thinking it would take some of the weight off my chest.

"What? How do you know? How do you even know it's mine? I knew I shouldn't have trusted you."

This, folks, is where it all began. All it took were those few words to send me into an indescribable rage, and now Richard had his ammunition that would follow us through our eighteen-year relationship. This was the first time I was gaslighted. I will never forget it.

We were no longer together after this phone call. I spent my pregnancy attending appointments alone, people hurling ugly stares because I was a young single mother with another one on the way. I felt ashamed that I had trusted this man, and I carried an immense amount of guilt that he did not want to be a part of his child's life. I hated myself for making poor choices for my children that they didn't deserve, and at the same time, I was excited that my little boy was going to be a big brother.

Richard's charm, however, is what reeled me right back in nearly seven months later. Well, his charm, and my desire to have a family that included the father of my child being present, and he knew this. I was raised in a single-parent household with a mother who worked three, sometimes four jobs at a time. I had always dreamed of being a great mother and having a partner who valued family as much as I did.

For the second time, motherhood was not working out the way I had dreamed it would.

When I was eight months pregnant and in the middle of moving to another apartment, Richard called my friend, who was helping me with the move. He knew she would answer the phone, and he knew if he asked for me, she would oblige. I reluctantly took the phone when she handed it to me. My gut was on fire with "don't do it" vibes. This became one of many pivotal moments where I didn't listen to my own intuition. I wanted a family for my children, and Richard said all of the right things.

The rest is a painful history.

Reflections

CHAPTER 2:

~

Idealization

I dealization is the first stage of the narcissistic cycle of abuse and often makes you feel like *this is too good to be true*. How could you possibly have met someone so much like you? A narcissist may pull the soulmate card, and if not, this is exactly where they are headed.

The truth is, they are nothing like you, which is why they chose you. A narcissist is actually empty inside. They have a fear of abandonment and/or rejection. They have carefully educated themselves on who you are so they could mirror you. Mirroring you is where you are left feeling as if the narcissist is just like you.

It begins with them asking you many questions about yourself. Social media makes this easier because if they have had access to your account, they already have an understanding of your likes or dislikes, how social you are or aren't, and have even looked up your friends and family to study your relationships. They study how you speak, your most commonly used phrases, and what makes you laugh - then they will take on these same or similar characteristics.

Asking all of these questions about you can feel flattering. They may have made you feel like they are genuinely interested in who you are. But I promise you, this is not the case. They are gathering information. This is where they learn how to be just like you. Using the same language, liking the same foods, movies, valuing the same character traits in people they even lie about having the same or similar life experiences to create a false sense of connection. This is what makes you believe you are perfect for each other.

Now, this is where the connection begins. A narcissist will start to tell you they have never known anyone like you. This can feel flattering, but let's be real - we are *all* unique. Of course, he hasn't met anyone just like you. They will find out what makes you feel good. If it's intelligence, they will sit in awe of you when you speak, comment on how intelligent you are, and ask questions to make you feel like they are genuinely interested in what you're talking about.

If it's your looks, prepare to be praised and worshipped. Narcissists will not only make you feel like you are the most beautiful person in the world, they'll often comment on how lucky they are. They'll compliment you when you get ready to go out, they'll even comment on wanting your future kids together to look just like you.

If your parenting is important to you, a narcissist will compliment you endlessly on your skills, commitment and relationship with your children. They'll ask for advice, tell you when they've used your advice, and comment on how it's worked out so well for them. Anything you hold valuable, and anything that is a weakness – they will use it to make you feel like they love you, flaws and all. They will sing your praises every chance they get.

Next, they will plan your future together. I mean, why wouldn't you want to plan to live the rest of your life with someone who is just like you?

Talk about marriage begins early in the relationship. A narcissist will talk about wanting to have children with you, moving in together, and building a life you have never imagined. That's if you've never imagined living with a monster, but we'll get to that later.

This fantasy they have gifted you is just that. It's not real, and it doesn't last. Once a narcissist has you deeply in love with the idea of them, they begin to pull back. Little by little, they'll begin to push boundaries. They'll stop calling you beautiful when you wake up in the morning (we all look like trolls when we wake up, and that's okay). They'll begin to challenge the things you talk about to subtly challenge your intelligence, and they'll question your loyalty towards them.

Much like an addiction, this creates a need to get back to that place that felt really good. You will begin to draw in closer to them, reconsidering things that you may have initially thought were too soon – like moving in together, marriage, or having a child. This is their plan from the beginning because once you commit through bills, a mortgage, a lease or children, they have you right where they want you.

If it feels too good to be true, it most definitely is.

I do believe that my first experience with narcissism when I was a teenager was that of an amateur, really. He was full of pride and disdain for himself. He didn't lay on the idealization too thick because, to be honest, he likely didn't know how, and he really didn't need to. I was young, alone, and the mother of a small child. I was an easy target.

As an adult, another experience was with a boss I had who was a raging, textbook narcissist. My car broke down, and I didn't have the money to have it repaired immediately. I was having a hard time getting to work, so he offered to buy me a car – just like that. He made this offer with a smirk, like he was making me an offer I couldn't resist. What he didn't know was that I had already caught on to his highly manipulative ways. Other employees had shared similar stories with me about him lending them absurd amounts of money and using it as leverage to threaten their jobs if they didn't comply with his demands. I declined, and quit that job as soon as I was able to move on.

My second narcissistic relationship experience was very well done. A narcissist at nineteen and a narcissist at forty have the same motives, but the lies the second one used to keep me from unmasking his manipulation were top-tier. Considering the second time I didn't make it out of the idealization stage before realizing who and what he was, I didn't get to see how long he could have kept it up. Because seriously, this stage can last for *years*. There will be some subtle slips and boundary testing along the way, but they can keep it up until they have you exactly where they want you. Trapped.

Reflections

CHAPTER 3:

~

Love-Bombing

It's exactly as it sounds. A narcissist will bomb you with acts of affection, attention, admiration, thoughtful or expensive gifts, and love.

It sounds nice, and to be honest, it feels wonderful at the beginning of the relationship. It's fun and exciting, it's nice to be seen and understood, and it's flattering to receive gifts and praise for no other reason than someone really likes to see you happy. The problem is, with a narcissist, it's a manipulation tactic they will use throughout your entire relationship. The purpose is to win you over and make you feel like they think you're special.

In the beginning, it can seem simple enough. Some will show up with your favourite snack, they'll remember your favourite lunch spot, or send flowers to your work. Some will be more lavish, but like most tactics a narcissist uses to hook you in, they will have a story to go with why they thought of you at that moment and were compelled to buy or send you something.

Love-bombing doesn't stop at gift-giving, though. It can be showering you with compliments or attention in the way of time or phone calls. They may want to spend a lot of time with you, want a commitment right away, or claim to love you very early in the relationship – like you're their soulmate. The way a narcissist love-bombs you will be specific to what they believe you hold most important to you. In my case, it was praise and acceptance. And let's be honest, we all want to be told we're beautiful by the person we are in a relationship with – so we can add that to the list as well.

Initially, It was subtle. Richard had a lot of pride, which made it feel even more special when he complimented me. But over time, he would withdraw the love and attention and replace it with anger or disgust in me. Richard would buy me expensive gifts and tell me how much I didn't deserve to have them. He often left the price tags on items and would comment about how hard he worked so he could provide me with nice things. And occasionally, he'd comment on how I didn't think of him as much as he thinks of me when shopping.

This constant push/pull of love/withdrawal causes us to crave the next good or loving moment. A narcissist creates experiences or moments that feel so good that we'll accept the alternating horrible times so we can return to the good again. Over time, I became so run down by Richard's demands when he complimented me (which by the end was never) or bought me things that I didn't even care for anymore. It's like being on a rollercoaster that's so much fun initially until you realize it isn't stopping and you want off.

Love-bombing is used for as long as it works. They will use any tactic to manipulate you to stay or to return after you've left them. They know what you like, so if it's time, they'll suddenly be available to you day and night. If you seek compliments, they'll compliment the hell out of you. If it's a connection, they'll insist that you are their soulmate and they can't go on without you. But as soon as a narcissist sees you comfortable and happy, they pull back. The overt abuse starts shortly after. They blame you for being annoying or clingy. They'll tell you they were mistaken, and maybe you aren't soulmates. They will even accuse you of making them spend money on you, and you'll be right back into the cycle of abuse.

Love-bombing is used with family members, your children, and anyone they can manipulate into praising them for their generosity, while their intent is to use the love-bomb as leverage for further abuse.

Reflections

CHAPTER 4:

~

Ghosting/Silent Treatment

G hosting and the silent treatment are common ways used to make you feel insignificant after he/she has given you all of their attention for an extended period. It's a way to devalue you and make you question if you've done something wrong. Often, it can make you feel like you are being punished. However, when their behaviour is addressed, they will often use the situation as a chance to accuse you of overreacting or being too clingy.

For many, ghosting happens at the end of the relationship when they just simply disappear with no logical explanation or closure.

I did not realize until long after I left Richard, that this was abusive behaviour. I really didn't know any better. I think it was a combination of being very young when we first began our relationship, paired with thinking that was just who and how Richard was.

When Richard and I first started dating, he was the most attentive person in my life. Not to be confused with offering excessive amounts of attention, which I would not have liked, but it's as if he knew when to be there for me and when I needed to be there for myself. He listened to what I had to say, and he claimed to understand me better than anyone else ever had.

Then he began disappearing. It started with a day here and a day there. Pride, being aloof, and not having a dependant nature caused me to ignore those days. He would eventually call and act like no time had passed, and we would go on with our relationship that was full of big laughs, fun moments, and the desire to be better for each other.

Those days would slowly turn into weeks at a time. When I would reluctantly address it, Richard would say, "Why are you always trying to be so clingy? I was busy. I was working." On other occasions, he would tell me he had tried calling me and that I was the one who was in fact ignoring his phone calls. He would then erupt in anger and deliberately ignore me until he decided his feelings were not hurt anymore.

Holidays and birthdays are the most common times for narcissistic men/women to disappear. It's all a part of the devaluing process often leading to a routine of them disappearing with no explanation. You're left to address that they were gone, only to be met with a fight. In turn, they would accuse you of overreacting or being clingy or controlling. You end up feeling like maybe you really were taking things a little too far, and you may have even gone as far as apologizing for ruining the holiday or birthday because of your behaviour.

The last year Richard and I were together, he ghosted me before his birthday. Mr. Charming always had the most over-the-top display for his birthdays, and I was given the responsibility as the planning leader (with his list of expectations) for the past seventeen years.

This year's birthday plans were no different in nature, other than I hadn't heard anything about any of it. Weeks before his birthday, I asked what the plan was, and if there was anything, in particular, he wanted to do. Richard's response was, "You should know what I like to do for my birthday. This is your job."

I later heard him on the phone with his brothers making plans to attend a specific party that was taking place on his birthday at a local club. Richard had been planning his own party all along, telling people I didn't want to attend or help out.

As the days got closer to his birthday, Richard began to come home after I had gone to bed, and he would leave for work unnecessarily early in the morning. When I did see him, he acted as if he was angry with me and ignored me. Richard started giving me dirty looks when he was home. In an attempt to intimidate me, he would slam doors, mumble, and swear under his breath when he saw me so I wouldn't question what his problem was. The air in the home became so thick with tension that everyone avoided being around him when he was home. He would leave with no explanation and return when he felt like it – often very late into the night.

The day before Richard's birthday, his brother called me to ask if I was driving to the event. I told him I was not informed of any event and I wasn't planning on going anywhere with any of them. At this point, I was so tired of being broken, used, and hurt. The unpredictability of his moods and rages had left me feeling I would never get any of it right, no matter what I did.

His brother, with a worried voice on the other end of the phone, said, "Don't do that. You have to come. You're his wife. Everyone is going to wonder where you are. You know how Richard is, he'll get over it, and you two will have a great night."

I hung up the phone and told myself that I would never spend another day feeling guilty for not showing up for someone who had no respect for me or my feelings. I didn't go, and I didn't care that I didn't go.

Richard yelled and called me an ungrateful whore. He accused me of wanting to see my *other boyfriend* instead. He told me I was a terrible wife and mother and that he should have known better than to marry a *white girl* like me – all in front of our children.

He had a modern day thirty-something-year-old temper tantrum. And I was over it.

Richard ignored me almost entirely for a solid month. He'd mumble obscenities under his breath when he saw me and called people to tell them lies about me loud enough that I could hear. If we had to cross paths, he'd stare at me like he wanted to kill me. If I asked him a question, he wouldn't even acknowledge me. Richard would look right past me as if I wasn't there, snicker and walk away.

Over time, I noticed that the silent treatment and ghosting weren't just for me. Richard treated everyone in his life he was close to like this as well. He had normalized this behaviour in his own family and circle of friends that everyone would just roll their eyes and say, "You know how he is."

Please know that this is abusive behaviour, no matter how normal their friends and family may want to pretend it is. The narcissist is devaluing you and trying to create an opportunity to control you by concocting a scenario where you are the bad guy. In the end, you'll need to oblige and apologize for something you didn't do.

If there is one thing I am grateful for now, it's that I am free from this relationship and free from all of this uncertainty.

Reflections

CHAPTER 5:

~

Devaluing

Once the narcissist has their hooks in you, they will begin devaluing you. This is who they really are at their core. Narcissists will start with mild insults they claim are just jokes. They will make you question your intentions in your relationship by making you feel like you are not good enough, and really, it's to feed their own ego and sense of entitlement at the expense of your self-worth.

This was what became the foundation of my relationship with Richard for many reasons:

1. He chose me so he could fuel his own sense of self, ego, and reputation. People love me. I'm funny, I'm a great parent, I'm nurturing, genuine, and intelligent. He wanted someone he could show up and show off with. I made him look good. The problem was, all of these things that caught his attention, he also hated me for.

2. He claimed to be a Christian man. Because he wanted to maintain this image, Richard needed me to stay with him, but be submissive. He needed me to be perfect in the eyes of everyone around us, but not so perfect that he would have to walk in my shadow.

Big shoes to fill, I know. It was many years before I realized how toxic and unrealistic this all was.

A few years into our relationship, Richard began spending more time at my place after our son was born – and the insults began. They were mild, indirect, and he often tried to play them off as a joke. Any time I would make a mistake or was wrong about something he would say, "See? You're not as smart as you think you are."

If I put on my favourite outfit, and he'd say, "You're not wearing that are you?"

Richard would tell me I wasn't funny after glaring at me from across a room while I was sharing jokes with friends. He would talk about other women in his family and imply that they were terrible mothers, then call me by their name with the most disgusted tone if I had made a mistake with one of my own children.

Over the years, these insults became a staple in our household. Once Richard and I moved in together, and he was more comfortable knowing I wasn't leaving, everything seemed to snowball. He began accusing me of sleeping with coworkers, neighbours, even his own family members. He would call me a whore if I brushed my hair before going to the grocery store. But If I didn't brush my hair before leaving the house with him, I was called worthless. He would regularly tell me I was stupid or not smart enough.

I began talking less, offering fewer opinions on anything and stopped trying to look presentable before leaving the house. My voice became quieter, and I laughed less when he was around. And if male family members came over, I would make myself busy with things that did not involve me having to be around any of them.

Early in our relationship, I had confessed some very personal and painful things about my childhood. At the time, Richard appeared so understanding and attentive. He made me feel safe.

Once we were living together, these confessions would come back to haunt me. In fits of rage, Richard would throw them back at me with such disgust in his voice. As much as I thought I was brushing off all of the indirect or soft insults, it wasn't until I was hit with the more direct accusations and opinions on who he said I was that I realized how broken I felt. I've never been much of a crier, which is why I think he found this so rewarding, but I would cry for hours. I sobbed until I would vomit – empty, hurt, and hating myself for trusting this one person with my secrets. He would tell me to shut up and call me a suck. Richard would say to me I had no reason to cry because *he* was the one having to live with such a disgraceful human being. If I had never known the power of words, I surely knew then.

I would wake up the next day to flowers, breakfast, and kids doing their homework or outside playing and laughing. I would literally wake up to the life I wanted. Nothing was ever addressed because I knew we would end up fighting again. So, I'd open my swollen eyes and force a smile when my kids presented me with a big glorious meal they had helped daddy to prepare just for me. I just wanted my children to be happy. That's what I kept telling myself. It was in these moments we had all learned this was literally how forever would be.

Later, when I had been worn down in the relationship, and Richard wasn't getting the desired response out of his insults, he began using intimacy as a tool to disrupt the peace at home.

One year, we were on vacation, on a beach, and we had the kids with us. He had been exceptionally mean to me throughout the day, and like I had been conditioned to do, I ignored it but felt run down no less. He insisted we go back to the hotel room to get our son's hat. Knowing he was going to want to be intimate, I asked him to go by himself. He glared at me in disgust, and I knew if I didn't go, we'd be trapped on a resort with him ruining everyone's vacation because he didn't get his way.

When we got to the room, he insisted we use this time away from the kids to be intimate. I told him I wasn't in the mood and wanted to get back to the children because I didn't feel right about leaving them. He persisted. I was uncomfortable but tried to play it off like I was okay with it, and we later left and went to tend to the children.

As we were walking down the hallway from the room he started. "You act like I raped you. You're my wife, you know, I have needs." I said, "Okay," and kept walking. Richard replied, "Men and women have roles. I'm not trying to pressure you into anything, but when you have a husband, you should want to tend to his needs." Again I replied "Okay" and kept walking. As I was walking down the hall of this beautiful resort, the rage ignited by his sense of entitlement got the best of me, and I turned to him and said, "I don't give a fuck who you are. If I say I don't want to sleep with you, *you* need to be okay with that." The look on his face was the first of many times I knew in my gut that he could kill me. I could feel the colour draining from my face. I kept walking so I wouldn't have to make eye contact with him. I knew the only reason why he wasn't exploding right now was because we were in a public place in another country.

For the rest of the day, Richard didn't speak to me as though I had done something wrong. The remainder of the week was riddled with 'you think I'm a rapist' comments and him exaggeratingly giving me more physical space than necessary. He even slept in the other bed with the kids.

This particular incident, along with others of this nature, came up until the day I left him. "You think I'm a rapist," along with "You must be sleeping with someone else, and that's why you don't want me," comments. Never for a second thinking that his entitlement to abuse his wife was the *real* turn-off.

As time went on, he found other more generic tools to devalue me. I had four beautiful children, and after having each one, my body changed. I gained weight, I lost weight, and I had stretch marks. These were all things Richard used to make sure I knew I was replaceable with someone younger, more physically fit, and who hadn't housed four humans.

He would never tell me I looked nice. Instead, he'd scowl at me as I got ready to go out or to work and say things like, "Pffft... who are you trying to look good for?" If I ignored his commentary, he would up the ante, answer his own derogatory questions, and get angry over things I did not say. Or, I'd smile and say, "For me." and leave it at that.

By the end of our relationship, Richard regularly told me that no man would want me because I was used, fat, and stupid. He drew on his opinion of me that I was too opinionated, loud, and annoying for anyone to want to be with me. He had convinced himself and everyone around him that I was leaving him for another man and that I was going to be sorry for leaving because this imaginary man would get sick of my shit too.

Reflections

CHAPTER 6:

~

Lying and Gaslighting

Lying and gaslighting are two different types of abusive behaviour but will often give each other the ammunition for either to work. They will make you feel like you are the unstable one who always overreacts in a situation. What later follows are feelings of guilt or an apology for something you haven't even done.

Here's the thing about these abusive men – they lie about everything and anything. They lie so much they believe their own lies, and they lie to cover the last lie so you will never really know the truth. I know in my case, Richard has never admitted to lying about anything, ever. He will stick to his story to the grave, which is what had me often wondering if I had really seen or heard what I had.

It wasn't until I was years out of the relationship, five books and years of reading deep into these abusive behavioural patterns, that I realized when things went missing in my home, it was because Richard took them and hid them.

Now, if you haven't been in this type of relationship, this may sound absurd. Which is precisely what I thought, even though it was happening to me.

Early in our relationship, I noticed Richard would wildly accuse his brothers of stealing his things. His clothing, car keys, money, and some of his other personal belongings. I remember thinking it was almost bizarre that he would think his brothers were always stealing his things. When I questioned him about it, he would tell me that I wouldn't understand because I didn't have siblings. Fair enough. I believed that this must be where the disconnect was.

So, when my own things went missing, I didn't question it. I have never been the most organized person, but I was not commonly in the habit of losing things. However, when my car keys would go missing, Richard would tell me that it was because I was forgetful. When my favourite nail polish disappeared into thin air, he would tell me that I must have thrown it out by accident.

Richard would accuse me of stealing or throwing out his belongings when he had misplaced them. They would always turn up, and then he'd accuse me of hiding them or putting them in a different spot to confuse him. This is something I always found particularly disturbing because why would I ever do something so strange?

There was a time my favourite shirt disappeared from its spot in my closet. There was nothing particularly phenomenal about this shirt other than it made me feel pretty. It was a Baby Phat t-shirt I had bought at a local Winners. It may have cost $15, but it was my go-to when I wanted to throw something on that was casual but flattering. I liked it, and he knew it.

Richard watched me look for it for hours. I checked the laundry, the washing machine, and the garbage. I took everything out of the closet, checked the cars, and even checked at work.

It was just gone.

About a year later, while looking for something completely unrelated, I grabbed a chair and pulled it up to the closet to check the top shelf. I'm short, so I could never reach or see what was up there. When I climbed up on the chair, you know what was there? My shirt. It was rolled up into a little ball and shoved in the back corner.

At the time, I knew in my gut that Richard had done this, but it seemed so far out of reality that I could not even bring myself to address it. So, I wore it. When he got home, he took one look at me and said absolutely nothing. Richard didn't even do a double-take. This was how good he was at trying to make me feel like I was losing my sense of reality.

Another time my son went on a trip with his father's side of the family to Disney World. Richard was jealous of this trip and of my son. The more excited my son got about the upcoming trip, the more Richard would say and do mean things to the point where my son stayed out of his way until his trip came.

When my son returned with all of his stories and souvenirs, Richard could not have acted more disinterested. One of the souvenirs my son had brought back was a plastic, oversized Mickey Mouse travel mug. My son wanted to use it at every meal. Until it disappeared.

This time I tore the house apart for this travel mug because I knew it had sentimental meaning for my son. I checked every garbage bin, under everyone's bed, even old boxes in the garage. It was just gone. When I asked Richard if he knew where it was or if he had seen it, he said it was in the cupboard – which was where I had put it last.

To this day, I know he took it and threw it out somewhere.

There may be a hundred stories of missing things over eighteen years. I still think it all sounds like it could not possibly be true, but I know it is only because I was there.

Richard would lie about where he was going, where he had been, and most of all, about other people. He always had something negative to say about someone when they weren't around. The conversation often started with 'you *don't know them like I do, they aren't who you think they are...*' I now realize he just did not want me to like or trust anyone.

Gaslighting however, is one of the most disturbing things I have ever experienced.

Being vehemently accused of doing or saying something you didn't do is a horrible form of emotional abuse. This attack on your character is an attempt to create chaos for *you* to be the one to blow up and lose your temper and for the other party to become the victim.

Sounds awful, right? That's because it is!

I have this one day etched into my brain. Most likely because I feel like I lost this fight by not remaining silent and because my children were present.

It was a Sunday afternoon, after church. Like always, we came home from the service starving, and I was quickly trying to throw together a meal for us and our four kids. I was tired, hungry, annoyed, and Richard knew it was a perfect opportunity to start something because my patience was short. I was in the kitchen, and he approached me, accusing me of not talking to him enough. He said, "Why don't you call me from work during the day and ask how I'm doing? Are you really at work? Why aren't you interested in what I'm doing? Other people's wives call to check-in. Why aren't you like them?"

There were two problems here. First, I ran a group home for teenage girls. This environment was unpredictable, sometimes violent, exhausting, and we didn't get any breaks, nor did we have any privacy to make these types of phone calls.

The second problem was, I just didn't give a shit. I worked hard and for long hours, and then I came home to my second job as a wife to a needy husband and four children. I wasn't going to call him from work simply because he would give me grief about something. Calling Richard would incite more anxiety about what kind of mood he would be in, than it would a chance to have a nice check-in.

This, of course, was not what I said to him, though, because I didn't want to feed his desire to fight. So instead, I said, "Listen, I'm hungry, tired, and annoyed. You sound like you're my fifteen-year-old-girlfriend right now. Can we talk about this another time?"

I'm not sure what I was thinking. I rarely spoke my mind with Richard because I knew he could kill me if he really wanted to. However, this day I was exhausted, and I was not having it. We had just spent two hours in church, talking and singing about kindness, love, and righteousness. Then I came home to be badgered by my husband while my kids groaned about being hungry in the next room.

Being an entire foot taller than I am, Richard stepped right up and over me. So close, I could feel his heart beating in his chest, smell his breath, and I could feel his fury. "What did you just say to me?" he growled. "Are you calling me gay?" Richard was trembling, and I was horrified that I let these words slip from my mouth when the kids were there. I knew better. I didn't know what would happen next, but whatever it was, I knew I didn't want my children to experience any of it.

"I was just joking," I said as calmly as I possibly could. It was too late. Richard started to push me back with his chest. He was in such a rage that I could feel the spit flying out of his mouth with every word. "You're calling me gay? You fucking white trash cunt!" I backed up as Richard was screaming, and I turned around and tried to run up the stairs. I was trembling and crying, terrified, begging him to stop following me. I ran into the washroom in our bedroom and slammed the door shut behind me, locking it.

Richard was still yelling at me, "You fuckin ungrateful, worthless white girl. You're nothing but white trash, I knew I shouldn't have married someone like you!" Then, with one shove, the bathroom door came flying in. He broke it, stepped in and over me again, shoving me with his chest so I would fall into the bathtub. He grabbed my arms to violently pull me away from the tub while calling me names.

Richard flung me with disgust onto the bed, and he went downstairs calmly, complaining in front of the children saying, "Mommy is in a bad mood." Richard then finished making their lunch and happily made a big production out of being happy, coming from church, and apologizing to them about *my* mood.

Richard later came back upstairs to tell me that everything was fine until I attacked him. He just wanted to be a good husband to me, but my attitude made it so difficult for him sometimes and that I should apologize when I am ready.

I was numb. Exhausted from coming down off that surge of adrenaline, and I had a migraine. But I promise you, I did not and would never apologize for Richard's uncontrollable rage.

Although the physical abuse in our relationship was sporadic - which is still dangerous, sporadic or not; the gaslighting was a regular occurrence, if not more frequent, when leading up to birthdays and holidays. I felt like I was regularly being accused of doing or saying things I didn't do or say, which caused me to speak less in general. The less I spoke, the fewer opinions I had, the quieter I became. I thought that would alleviate some of the abuse.

Even during his best performances, I always had a clear understanding that I was not to blame for his anger, but I just could not justify leaving him and breaking up our family. Richard somehow made himself the victim in every single scenario. Something in me felt he needed me to be there for him, because he felt he was being victimized by the world.

The thing about narcissists is they can tell lies without being caught because they believe them. There are no telltale signs of lying. No nervousness, identifying eye movements –nothing. They have also learned to cover their lies with more lies and create scenarios that will make you feel sorry for them, even when you catch them in a lie.

They will surely be angry with you for catching them in a lie, and more so for asking them about the lie. Imagine, they get angry at you for addressing their lies?

Here's the thing about lies and narcissists – the lies are like cockroaches. Where there is one, there are hundreds.

Reflections

CHAPTER 7:

~

Isolation

In a narcissistic or any abusive relationship, for that matter, the abuser needs to isolate you from friends and family, so they are your only source of connection to the outside world. This way, they can control your thoughts about yourself and the world around you. It also creates a dependency on them for company, money, access to a vehicle, and it removes anything or anyone that could help you to leave them.

My first experience with Richard isolating me from friends went like this... When I met him, I already had an existing group of friends with whom I had spent a lot of time. Most were young men, and my friendships with them were entirely platonic. This was a problem for Richard, and nothing was overtly said in the beginning, but his body language, the tone of his voice – everything told me he was jealous. However, being in high school, I thought this was normal, flattering even.

Over time, when I would spend time with them, I would hear less from Richard. He would ignore my calls or disappear entirely for days. But If I spent more time with him and less with my friends, then I would see him more, and he would attend to my needs and wants. So naturally, I spent more and more time with Richard.

Christmas rolled around. We had been together on and off for two years. One of my male friends called me to wish us all a Merry Christmas and I had him on speakerphone. This friend made a (very innocent teenage boy) joke about my panties. It was a completely non offensive joke, but Richard's face changed at that moment. Suddenly, it was so tense I could feel the room fill up with his negative energy. I hung up the phone, and Richard proceeded to accusingly ask me if I was sleeping with my friend. I insisted I wasn't and was confused, as the joke really was innocent.

Richard wouldn't let it go. He got up, dramatically handed back the Christmas gift I had bought him, and left me sitting there on Christmas Day with the kids. Richard was gone. He didn't answer his phone for a week. I didn't hear from him or see him until he showed up a week later, demanding to see his son. Richard proceeded to tell me it had to be him or my friends and that he would not continue his relationship with me if I remained in contact with this group of friends.

We had a baby together, and although I told him this was an unfair decision to have to make, I reluctantly and silently avoided speaking with them.

When we would visit my mothers family, albeit sporadically since my family is not close, he would claim to be uncomfortable around them. He would accuse my uncles of making racist remarks in front of him, which could have been true, although I had never witnessed this. I do know my one side of the family to have some actively racist members. So, without a fuss or a question, we spent less time with my family.

When I met Richard in high school, I had more friends than I can count. I'm charismatic and funny, so people love me. Little by little, I became alienated from most of them, or at the very least, I distanced myself from them to keep the peace at home.

Don't forget, this all begins subtly. For me, it started with my male friendships. Sometimes our mutual friends would come over to hang out with everyone, and a few days later, he'd say something like, "I saw how he looks at you. He's in love with you." I'd insist that this wasn't true and give examples of why it could never be true. I would even go to lengths to prove that the friend was interested in someone else. I would exert all of this energy to prove something that didn't happen. Sounds exhausting, right? But this was just the beginning.

Over time, he would insist that I had slept with my friends (and his friends) or that I was currently sleeping with them. We would fight, and I would cry. I just stopped allowing myself to be in their presence.

Then it was time to dismantle my female friendships. This took more energy on Richards's part, but you had better believe it started with him accusing me of wanting a same-sex relationship with certain friends. When this didn't work because I found no offence in being called Queer, he'd move on to what he believed to be issues with their character.

I have always deeply valued my female friendships and took great pride in my girlfriends being incredible humans. Over time, he would accuse my friends of flirting with him, of cheating on their husbands and of being terrible mothers. Then to seal the deal, he would compare me to them.

You see, the psychological game here was for Richard to discredit and devalue these women, and then tell me I must be just like them – which he had hoped would make me distance myself from them.

"So and so is cheating on her husband. You must want to be friends with her because you are too."

"So and so never wants to parent her own kids, that's why their kids are always here. Why don't you just go out with her too and leave your kids behind. I know that's what you want."

"So and so thinks she knows everything, just like you. You two think you're so smart, and I can't stand it when she's here because you're worse when she's around."

We went to a family Christmas party one year with my mother's side of the family. My uncle's wife's brother hosted. He had a big flashy house and all the expensive things that go along with it. He was also a hyper-masculine alpha male.

I can tell you that this ended up being the worst Christmas ever. My ex was so uncomfortable and angry from the moment we stepped foot in that home, and he made us all pay for it as soon as we got in the car to leave. He accused this man of being racist with zero indication of this. I know this because it was the only time we had been in contact with said person. Richard hated how he doted over the children and me. Perhaps, he too, was a narcissist, but whatever it was, the outcome was awful. This man had given beautiful gifts to the children, including money. All of which Richard berated the children for receiving the entire drive home. Next morning, the money the children were so happy to have received was gone. Richard took their gifted money because he felt entitled to everything the children owned, and he was angry that another man had made them happy without his permission.

Richard used this experience against me for years. He would bring it up by accusing me of flirting with this man, for not defending him when this man was looking down on him (which, again, I did not witness), and allowing the kids to enjoy their time there. I promise you, the thought of ever returning to this man's home made me physically ill. So we didn't. If this meant we would miss Christmas dinner with my immediate family, that would be the decision that would have to be made.

Whatever friends I did have left, Richard carefully chose which ones would stay, and he would work on which ones would not. He would accuse my friends of being promiscuous (which they weren't) and go as far as lying, saying they had tried to sleep with his friends or cousins. Also, untrue. Richard would sometimes insist that I was better than they were and that if we were going to make this relationship work, we both had to make some sacrifices to be better together.

This was when I started to become friends with his family and friends. Slowly, systematically, Richard managed to have me slip away from many of my friends. Over the next sixteen years, Richard's family became my family, and his friends became my friends. This transition made leaving him in the end so agonizing. I was not just leaving him. I was leaving everyone who had become so important to me.

Having me isolated from those who saw Richard for who he really was and who would have encouraged me to leave him was what ultimately kept me in this relationship. His *friends* and family were the ones who tolerated him the most. I learned over time that many of them wanted me there, so he would leave them alone. I'll leave *friends* in italics because narcissists do not really have any friends – they have followers, also known as enablers and flying monkeys. They will only keep people in their friendship and family circle who enable their behaviour.

The truth is, the narcissist you may be with right now has chosen you because there is something great that he/she sees in you. Whether it's charisma, the capacity to love others, intelligence, kindness, tenacity or resilience – these are things he sees in you that he/she wishes they had. Naturally, these are the things others see in you and love about you. So the narcissist wants to destroy these qualities in you.

The longer you are in this relationship, the more control he/she asserts. This means he/she has had more time to groom you and eradicate your powerful friendships and relationships with others.

Looking back, I can't believe how ridiculous and calculated this all was. However, at the moment when all I wanted to do was survive, to keep the peace, and for Richard to stop making me feel small – I shut my mouth, telling myself that I was not going to argue with him over my friends. When really, I was affirming his power over me and subconsciously distancing myself from the friendships that would hold me up.

I did, however, still have the illusion of having many friends. He had an enormous family of enablers, and had *friendships* consisting of people (mostly women) who worshipped the ground he walked on. At the time, I thought these were my people too. They saw what he did. Many knew he was abusing us, and they made the same excuses for Richard that I did. They gave the illusion of love and support to my children and me, but when the shit hit the fan, you had better believe I was standing alone.

By the time I decided to tell him I was leaving, I had very few solid friendships left. The ones that I did have had no idea we were being abused. The rest were his people, and he forced them to fiercely choose sides.

Isolation is not limited to family and friendships either. Limiting your spending, berating your decisions to take care of yourself, and restricting movement by hiding car keys, or making you feel like leaving the house could cause increased violence in the home - are all examples of isolation.

I always tell young women if there are signs of an uneven power dynamic, and he says he wants you to have his children and be a stay-at-home mother – run. He's telling you he wants all of the control in the relationship.

Reflections

CHAPTER 8:

~

Breaking You Down

B reaking you down goes hand in hand with devaluing you. It is much like being a prisoner, but the narcissist gives you the shackles to place on yourself. And because you likely believe that this is what you deserve, they hold the key. They make you feel worthless and that you are lucky to have them tolerate you. I learned the hard way that subjecting myself to Richard's authoritative ways also meant he meticulously controlled how I felt about myself. Like many of you, I was a confident and well-liked young woman. I had a large group of friends, people were always happy to see me, and they thought I was interesting and intelligent.

These are all the things that drew him to me. I made Richard look good. However, these were also things he hated the most about me because they were areas he lacked in his image of himself.

Like all of the other red flags, this stage began so subtly. A comment about a new haircut, a pair of pants being too tight, questioning my ability to make decisions and so on. What I didn't realize was that these questions over time would cause me to question myself.

Did he outright call me fat? No, not in the beginning. That would be an obvious sign of trouble, and it would allow me to point my finger at him and question his intentions. Instead, he would sit and watch me get dressed and say, "You're not wearing that are you? I think you need a bigger size." I know it sounds innocent enough, but when it's your favourite outfit that fits well and is likely something someone has complimented you on, then it's one of those subtle comments that becomes the piece of a much bigger picture.

One or two *(un)helpful* comments about my size is not where it ended either. To put it into context, I was a size 6 at the time. Richard would begin to say things regularly like:

"So, are you happy with that size or... maybe we should get a gym membership."

"Are you sure you're not pregnant again?"

"You can't wear that in public."

"I think you should have bought a bigger size."

"Are you sure you need that piece of cake?"

"I didn't put any carbs on your dinner plate because I figured you were trying to cut down."

When we got closer to the end of the relationship, he'd flat out tell me no man would ever want me because I was used and overweight. If it wasn't the weight issue, he often told me that I wasn't as smart as I thought. If I made a decision, he would tell me that it didn't make sense, even if I was simply choosing between pink or red throw pillows. Over time, I learned to doubt myself entirely. I either refused to make any decisions, which gave Richard all the power in the decision-making, or I would nervously make an easy decision and wait to see if he approved or if he would berate me for doing something *so stupid*.

He absolutely hated that people found me witty or funny. One of the times he struck me was after he walked in on me, making a room full of people laugh. Richard often told me that I wasn't funny, but that he thought I was rude. I pushed back by telling him if people were laughing, they must find what I'm saying amusing. He did not. And the angrier he got and the quieter I became.

We were at a friend's house this particular night, and Richard had spent most of the evening in the garage with the other men. I had remained inside with everyone else. He walked in just as I was finishing a story, and the room erupted in laughter. I looked up at him, and he was scowling at me as he walked by. It was at that moment, I knew things were not going to be okay. I felt like I had rocks in the pit of my stomach, and my throat was closing. On the verge of panic and tears, I went to the washroom to gather myself and re-enter the room as if nothing was wrong.

That night when we got home, Richard was in a rage, scream-ing that I had embarrassed him, and how my disrespectful be-haviour was something I should be ashamed of. I was terrified as he became increasingly louder and more irrational. It felt like the more I attempted to ignore his hysteria, the more aggressive he became. Like clockwork, I began to cry, and the more I cried, the worse it was. He would mock me, blame me for his violence, and somehow turn himself into the victim.

For those of you who know the shame in wearing long sleeves to work in the summer, you know this night ended with horrific results. It was days like these that broke me. I spoke less and less when people were around, trying to make myself smaller in his presence. All of the things I loved about myself were carefully tucked away so he wouldn't be angry with me so often.

By the end of our relationship, I was filled with body image issues, shame, self-doubt, the inability to make decisions, feeling like I wasn't smart enough, and an intense feeling of powerless-ness that continues to take work and so many years to attempt to rectify.

What I still had, though, was the ability to make people laugh, especially at his expense. Some will call it petty, but I know that my ability to make light of all of this is what kept me from crumbling.

Truth is, now that I've been on this journey of healing and reflection, I don't even think about Richard enough to make any jokes about him at all. I'm on my path to never think about him or our relationship ever again, and this is where I'd love for you to be as well.

Reflections

CHAPTER 9:

~

Control

Gaining total control of you as a person is a narcissist's ultimate goal. Once they have complete control, they have full-time access to someone to manipulate and abuse. This is the only way a narcissist feels anything, and it is this power that drives them to continue to abuse/control you.

Control in this relationship was the foundation of all the other abuses that took place. Like every other red flag, it took years of subtleties, small acts, and the guise of being overprotective for me to realize I no longer had any control over anything that was happening in my home.

When Richard and I met, we were still young, so things like parties and clubs were our method of entertainment. There was a time we were at a club having what I thought was a great time. A man approached me and leaned over to ask me what time it was. The next thing I knew, Richard's hand reached across and grabbed this man by the collar of his shirt. I immediately insisted this man had only asked me for the time. The man was released, and Richard apologized. I'll admit, at the time, I thought this was flattering.

Richard later explained that he was *just overprotective,* and I liked it. Until the fifth, sixth and seventh time, he started to accuse me of intentionally getting the attention of other men. By the end of our relationship, if we were at a club or a party, Richard would always accuse me of going to the washroom so I could talk to other men.

His purpose behind this? Richard didn't want me to go out to parties anymore, and it worked. If I would go out with my girlfriends and knew what to expect because once I was home, he would accuse me of cheating while I was out.

The good old silent treatment was another passive form of control. Richard could go days or even weeks not speaking to me. It was as if he was punishing me by invalidating my wants and me as a person. There was a day I overheard Richard talking with a woman on the phone, and I knew it was a woman because I could hear her voice. They were laughing and talking for what felt like a long time, and Richard got up from the living room to walk to the garage to continue his conversation when I heard him say, "No, she's just my baby-mother, and I pay her."

I was crushed and irate. So, when Richard finished his conversation and came back inside, I asked him who he was speaking to. He immediately erupted into a rage. The more I insistently repeated what I heard him say, Richard called me a liar. He said he was done talking and didn't speak to me or acknowledge me for over a week. There was no communication. Just dirty looks, muttering things under his breath and completely ignoring anything I said to him.

When he decided we would talk again, he laid on all the love and attention I had missed out on with lots of hugs and goofiness. If I wanted to address Richard's conversation with that woman again, he would accuse me of trying to cause more problems between us. I would again have to work through the possibility of being ignored and devalued for weeks.

After several incidents like this, I learned to become desperate for Richard's attention while simultaneously not wanting to draw attention to myself. I wanted his pleasant side and attention, but was also afraid he would show up as angry Richard. I stopped addressing most things. I stopped challenging him, and I stopped communicating my own feelings.

Another method of narcissistic control Richard used, probably the most, was with his body language and dominating stance. He is a very tall man, an entire foot taller than I am, so he would use his size to intimidate me. It was a reminder that Richard was much bigger and stronger than I was. When his behaviour began to escalate and become aggressive, I knew that he was inching towards violence as he physically moved closer to me. Sometimes, he even pushed me into walls and furniture with his body. I can still feel his presence to this day. Even in a sea of hundreds of people, I can feel him taking up all the space in a room. This is why I make every effort not to be in the same space as he is, even almost a decade later.

Then there is the cold stare. Anyone who has known a narcissist knows this look. It's one that most people on the outside of his household won't be able to identify, but it feels like he's looking into your soul. Richard would glare at me with disgust, and I knew something chaotic was going to happen later. That look would make my skin crawl. It could be so subtle that others would not notice, but it would fill me with fear.

To solidify his disinterest in me, Richard would often appear to be really loving, kind or accepting to someone else in my presence or over the phone. This was how he would indirectly show me how disinterested he was in me.

There are endless ways narcissists can gain control over you and how you can position yourself in this relationship. For the sake of not writing out an example of every incident I had experienced, because there are so many, I'll leave you with a list for clarification.

A narcissist will play the victim and exaggerate the suffering they have experienced in their own history of abuse, loss, grief, or disappointment. Many have suffered real loss and have experienced one or several traumatic events as children. However, it is not uncommon for them to exaggerate events or completely lie to garner your sympathy. They will even go as far as lying about being in car accidents or losing friends or family members to disease. Most commonly, they will insist that previous relationships were abusive towards them, and say that their ex-partner's have cheated on them or hurt them in other ways.

Much of what they share are lies or stories in which they have hurt others but will turn it into a narrative where they are the actual victim. This is how they can manipulate your empathy and create an environment where you think they need you to feel safe or loved. A narcissist will compare you to others, making you believe someone else is better than you and that you aren't good enough for them. This leads you to the belief that you are lucky to have them.

Narcissists will deny your reality, so they can evade taking responsibility for actions that have caused you to feel guilt or shame. It's common for them to say they are the ones who are hurt while watching you exhaust yourself trying to find solutions. It is as if they are upset with you because they made you upset.

Narcissists have no real sense of humour. His or her humour always comes at the expense of someone else. They will mock you in front of others about your appearance or something you did (that they know would be embarrassing for you) and follow it with '*I was just joking.*' They feel entitled to point out your weak spots while claiming they are just being honest. Your feelings of shame in front of others will allow them to manipulate an environment where you will do anything to make yourself small around other people. They will also make fun of your hobbies or passions. This is how they control your emotions and create insecurities.

Narcissists will coordinate reactive abuse. This means they will accuse you of saying or doing something you did not do (gaslighting). Often, it reflects what you are proud of or sensitive about, like your values or your character. They will keep pushing and pushing until you explode. Afterwards, they will accuse you of being the abusive one. This form of coercion always leaves victims feeling like perpetrators, and a narcissist will bring up these events later to show you how they are actually *your* victim.

Reflections

CHAPTER 10:

⁓

Projection

Narcissists use projection as a means of gaslighting. They will accuse you of doing, believing, or saying something that is totally out of your realm of possibilities. We should keep in mind that most of what they are projecting onto you is their own behaviour, belief, or something they have said or done to others.

How many times have you been accused of doing or saying something that has never actually happened? Something that sounds so ridiculous you'd almost want to laugh, but the basis of what you are being accused of isn't funny? I have learned over the years that I was often accused of doing things I would never do, but it was likely Richard would/had.

Let me explain. There was a point in our relationship that I worked rotating shifts, mothering four small children and doing sports runs, all while maintaining a well-run household. With that being said, I barely had time to breathe but was often accused of cheating.

To put things into perspective, I was exhausted emotionally and physically. I had an abusive husband and became increasingly distrustful of men. Nor was I interested in them as a species. The *last* thing on my mind was engaging another man in any sort of activity when I did not even want the one I had.

I was violently accused of cheating regularly. I was accused of lying about working so much that Richard would call my workplace to see if I was there. He even went as far as driving by to see if my car was in the parking lot. If I were out for lunch, he would call my cell phone and ask where I was. I later discovered that Richard knew the password to my phone. He would check my messages and social media when I was in the shower. I also have reason to believe that he had somehow tapped the landline (an old school phone) to record my conversations.

There was a time I had gone for lunch with a close friend who I had not seen in a year. Hours passed as we talked and caught up on our busy lives, laughing, reminiscing...all the things you do with good girlfriends. After around two hours, the string of text messages started. Richard wanted to know why I had not come home yet. He wanted me to call him. Richard finally became so angry, he told me not to bother coming home and that he and the kids were fine without me. He was essentially telling me not to return home, ever.

I eventually called Richard because his messages were upsetting me, and I didn't want my friend to catch on that something wasn't right. He immediately began berating me, telling me I was a whore and he should have known better than to marry a cheater like me.

All because I was having a nice lunch with my friend.

What I later discovered was Richard projected what he was really doing onto me. He hated himself and hated that he thought I was a better person than he was. So he felt compelled to project his hurtful ways and insecurities onto me. Thus, making himself feel superior to me at that moment.

Richard would regularly accuse me of cheating when he was the one who was cheating. Richard often accused me of lying when he was the one who would lie – about everything. He would accuse me of hiding his things, like his keys or his clothing. Both being items of mine that would occasionally disappear and reappear weeks later. He would accuse me of being mean or selfish when every waking moment of my life was spent in service to others.

Richard accused me of being the abuser in the relationship. The days he would push me into a rage was his favourite time to shine. Richard would call his family and tell them how he tolerated my temper and moods. He would even refer back to these moments when speaking in front of the children so they would begin to think I was the aggressor.

These accusations were additional ways in which Richard tore away at my self-esteem. I was often left wondering if maybe I had said or done something that would lead him to think these horrible things about me. I found myself constantly trying to defend my character, and he would use those opportunities to further damage the way I felt about myself. He would say things like, "I always knew I couldn't trust a ghetto girl like you." "I can't believe you're cheating on me, and you're the mother of my children." Or "Next time, I'm going to marry a woman who understands my culture, so I don't have to put up with this." And finally, "You need help."

As I write this, I can still feel my shoulders and neck tense up. The confusion and desperate need to be heard yet feeling as if I was talking to a wall. The culmination of frustration and sadness that my husband thought of me as being *this* person. I now know that all of this was to feed his own suffering ego.

When a narcissist accuses you of affairs out of your character, you will find these are the things they are doing – *if* you look hard enough.

You know the saying, "It's not you, it's me?"

When referring to a narcissist it's, "It's not me, it's you."

Reflections

CHAPTER 11:

~

Financial/Economic Abuse

F inancial abuse is a concept that has become identified more recently as a form of abuse. Financial abuse is a way to control your finances and credit, leaving you dependent on the narcissist, so it becomes almost impossible to leave the relationship. Or, for some, it does become impossible to break away. Women with children are more likely to be poorer if they leave an abusive home. We stay to avoid poverty. It's survival.

Does financial abuse mean you are handing all of your money over to them? *No.* It means the narcissist has manipulated you over time with small steps to leave you with less control over your finances, thus giving them more access to your money along with more money for himself to save or spend.

This was something I did not even know was possible until many years after I left. I was made to believe my bankruptcy, lack of credit, non-existent insurance history, and inability to maintain our lifestyle after leaving were my fault.

There were so many signs. I thought they were all decisions married people made because I did not know or understand this at the time. Through research, talking with other women who have lived in similar circumstances and doing some honest reflection on how I had reached this point, I realized that there was an actual method to what had taken place, which falls under the same categories of control and isolation.

When a narcissist can control your finances, they control all other aspects of your life, even after you have left.

It started with indirectly asking me or making me offer to spend my money on him.

Here's a scenario. You go shopping, and they pick up something they really like. They look at the price tag and put it back looking slightly disappointed. Generally, this can be the behaviour of any of us. What makes this different is that they would bring it up again after a really great night. Or the narcissist would say something to the effect of, "My birthday is coming up. I really loved that 'thing'. I hope someone buys it for me."

Sold.

I wanted Richard to be happy, but there was no end to this. He would increasingly find ways to spend my money on him so I would have less for myself, and his bank account would continue to grow or be available for his own frivolous spending.

What started out as the occasional article of clothing turned into the bills, the mortgage, elaborate parties, the roof on our home, the windows, the speakers in his car, his student loans, family trips, increased credit limits – and I could go on and on. What really hurt me financially is most of this went onto my own credit, which I eventually could not repay.

The result? He had lots of nice things, and I had a bankruptcy. This bankruptcy made it impossible for me to obtain credit after leaving him, including car loans or a mortgage. What was even worse, I could not find a rental property for my kids and me because I had terrible credit.

However, this reality is a whole other book in itself.

I realized over the years Richard was not only spending my money, but he was spending other family members' and our children's money.

The kids would get money for their birthday, and Richard would take it and spend it on groceries to avoid using his own money. Once the kids were old enough to work, he would have them spend their money on him while reminding them of all the times he had done the same for them. He has borrowed large amounts of money from family with no intention of paying them back, and made them feel guilty about asking when he would repay it.

Narcissists feel entitled to everything their significant other and children have. They believe we are all their property, and we all owe them our soul in exchange for them being a parent or a partner.

When we were first married, Richard insisted we have a joint bank account. This may have been the one, and only time I listened to my gut and refused. He would scream at me saying this is what married couples do and I was embarrassing him. My response was always, "You will never question my spending when I work just as much as you do." I never wavered from this. I even felt powerful, but I did not realize he found other ways for me to hand my money over to him.

My mother and my grandmother often relayed to me, "You should always have a bank account your husband doesn't know about. Even if you put in $10 a paycheque, there will come a day that you will need this money. Whether it's to plan an escape or go on a vacation, don't shortchange yourself with this idea that he isn't doing the same or that you will never need it."

I still wish I had listened to this advice. By the time I was ready to leave, I had nothing – no money, no credit, and no ability to secure a safe space for us to live.

I cannot stress this enough. Hide money if you can. I know some of you are completely controlled financially. Even as far as being kept from working so you have to ask for money, but if you can – do not make the same mistakes I did.

If right now you are in a position to plan your exit strategy, even If you are not working or making so little money that you would be eligible for social assistance, you may qualify for financial support in the courts. Take all the assistance and free support you can!

The problem I ran into in accessing free support was that I had four dependent children and worked full time. I barely made enough for us to survive, but I could not access any financial assistance to help with court costs. This was a costly setback not only financially but also emotionally for us all. This is certainly an incident where I had wished I had access to money he did not know about.

When and if you are planning to exit, make sure you consult with a lawyer. There are services in many cities that offer free consultations. And please, when you consult with a lawyer, make sure they specialize in domestic violence, even if he has never hit you. In addition, always remember that just because a service is free or low cost does not mean you need to settle for anyone who will hear you out.

When people want to help you, let them. Maybe it's a place to stay. It could be with some groceries, childcare, emotional support at court, clothing – whatever it is. Now is not the time to let your pride get in the way. I could not have done this without the help of my friends and family, who made sure we had food and a safe place to stay, even when I was too tired to ask for it.

I had a friend who would come at night and drop grocery gift cards in the mailbox without a word. He never asked. I never told him much. I will never forget this because he didn't know that at the time, I was missing meals so my kids could eat.

Here is the bottom line; financial abuse comes in many subtle forms:

Making you feel guilty for not purchasing things for him.

Leaving you to make all of the purchases concerning the children.

Making large withdrawals from a joint bank account.

Questioning you with the intent of controlling your spending.

Putting all of the bills in your name.

Putting his business in your name (this leaves you legally responsible financially if he decides to walk away).

Refusing to contribute to the household expenses.

Stealing your credit card or debit card to make purchases.

Taking your money or the children's money without asking.

Accusing you of selfishly spending on yourself and not spending on him.

Not adding you as a beneficiary on insurance while he is the beneficiary on yours.

Not adding you to insurance plans.

Having access to credit in your name.

Hiding his income and expenses.

Expecting you to cover the cost of large purchases through manipulation.

Breaking your phone or other necessary items knowing you do not have the money to replace them.

Closing bank accounts without consulting you.

Refusing to pay child or spousal support.

There may be two on the list that you can resonate with, or there may be twenty. The point is, financial abuse is abuse, and it is crucial to be able to recognize these signs.

Reflections

CHAPTER 12:

~

Triangulation

Triangulation is a way a narcissist attempts to control the interpretation or understanding of communication between two people or two groups of people. The narcissist will try to ensure communication goes through them first before reaching the other party to inflate their importance and make themselves feel powerful.

Narcissists use lies, secrets, manipulation, and your insecurities to cause someone else (or a group of people) to dislike you or believe you are the abuser. Alternatively, they may lead others to believe they are with you out of pity by concocting stories about your failing finances, living arrangements, health, mental wellness etc.

These narcissists triangulate to remain in control of what other people think of you while making their own fragile self look and feel better. Abusers are often empty inside, and this is what fuels their need to gain power by making you look like you are not as great as people think you are.

Early in my relationship with Richard, when we were still just friends, he spoke a lot about his ex-girlfriend. He would tell me how she broke his heart by cheating on him and would insist she was his first love.

To be honest, I didn't care.

When Richard did not receive the expected reaction, he began detouring when we were out driving. The detour was to her house. We would drive by, and he would outwardly reminisce about their relationship, and glance over at me to see my reaction. I could not have been more disinterested. At the time, I thought he was atten-tion-seeking – so I chose to not give in.

Several years later, while we were at a party, his ex-girlfriend showed up with her boyfriend. I was not aware he had invited her, and he was overly excited to introduce us. My friends were irritated by this, but I happily walked over and introduced myself.

Richard ignored me for the remainder of the party.

When we arrived home, Richard angrily told me I had embar-rassed him with my rudeness and I was jealous of his ex-girlfriend. I insisted I never would have done anything to spite her. I did not know her or care that they were once in a relationship. Richard continuously spoke over me, insisting I was rude and embarrass-ing. I'm sure the story he told her was equally untrue, and I am positive he apologetically told her and his friends that I was jealous of her.

This triangulation continued and increased in frequency over the years we were together.

I additionally noticed this with Richard's female friends, who I did not know very well. Most were coworkers, and he made it a point to keep me separate from his work friends. Richard never invited me to attend a work function. Instead, he always brought his cousin.

On occasion, when I did meet someone from his work, she would be cold or aloof. I didn't question this initially, and I couldn't put a finger on their reaction towards me until the end of our relationship. Richard had this group of coworkers who acted as if the sun rose and set on him. They hung onto every word he said, laughed at every joke he made (and I promise you, Richard is not *that* funny), and they catered to him as if he was a king. I know this because he would spend endless hours on the phone with them, sometimes on speakerphone so I could hear, although he would never invite me to be a part of the conversation.

One time, Richard started a fight with me in the days leading up to New Year's Eve, as he had always done over the holidays. I was particularly annoyed because he went out of his way to tell me how much he did not want me there, and I now was in a foul mood. I bumped into one of his female coworkers in the wash-room, who Richard introduced to me that evening. I only knew who she was because he spoke on the phone loudly with her often. She leaned in really close and said, "You are *so lucky* to have a man like Richard. Especially since he's raising a child who's not his."

Huh?

It had been years since I wanted to fight someone. That day I almost let years of rage explode onto someone else. With a fire in my belly, a red face and not even a blink, I walked away from her.

I did not address this with Richard. However, the fact that this still sits in my memory bank reminds me of how significant the moment was. I later learned Richard had been telling his work friends I was so ungrateful, and I mistreated him, when all he wanted was a loving wife and family. He spoke about how hard it was for him to raise my eldest – who was not his biological child. He had created the most untrue scenario in the minds of others at my expense.

Richard would often speak about scenarios that never happened while with the children. He would try to plant words or things I had done to hurt him (that never actually happened) and create a picture of me in their minds as an instigator. He would call people and speak loudly on the phone for hours about how mean or spiteful I was and how everyone didn't know the *real Mirlo.*

I later realized some things he would say about me to others were lies, and they were incidents he had done or said to me. He hated that others liked me and would take personal offence to this. It was as if their fondness of me meant they enjoyed him less. Everything was a competition with Richard. In his mind, there was no possible way we could both be great. In order for him to be great, I needed to be a burden in the eyes of others so he could appear to be my saviour.

Triangulation was, and still is, used amongst the children as well. He was jealous of them and their relationship with me, and especially their relationships with each other. He used a triangulation tactic to berate my young sons for coming to me for comfort when they were hurt or upset. If Richard saw them come to me instead of him, he would yell, "Get away from your mother! She can't help you. What kind of pussy runs to their mother for everything?"

This conditioned the kids to force themselves either to approach him for pseudo-comfort or to internalize their pain. They also did not trust that I was a person who provided safety. The children became afraid to show me any kind of affection, especially in front of Richard or his family.

Another tactic Richard would use was to lie about one child's behaviour in the presence of another. This was how he would attempt to keep them from becoming too close to each other. Richard would say one of the children was so rude towards him all the time and he would act as if he was having such a hard time with this because he wanted to be a good parent. He would often accuse me of brainwashing the kids so they would love me more, and in turn, he would accuse them of being disrespectful towards him. Which, of course, they never were, out of fear of him.

He wanted them to feel confused and unclear about their own loyalties and make himself the victim of every person in the household so he could choose one child to praise for their love and devotion to him. This would make that child his favourite, or the Golden Child.

The child who was rarely home to witness what was happening would side with Richard, which was easy to do because the children craved his praise. This caused the child who was rarely home to feel a sense of protection for their father from the rude or disrespectful sibling used as a scapegoat. Now, the two children involved are not as close as they once were. Classic divide and conquer.

Not only does this create a very unhealthy dynamic in the home, but it also empowers the abuser to continue abusing and triangulating to remain in power. A narcissist will now have to maintain this image of being superior to his/her peers while dominating their family and looking like they are the victims in their household.

Does it sound confusing? This is because it is.

I learned near the end to use a response without a reaction as a mode of survival. I did not address everything because that would continue to allow Richard to create chaos. However, if I could safely elicit a response without emotional reciprocation, I would. I still do when it comes to the children, but for the most part, I have absolutely no contact with him at all.

His use of triangulation laid the groundwork for conflict and chaos, and Richard was in control of it all. Whether the battles were between him and me, him and the kids, the kids with each other, or the kids and myself, it did not matter. What mattered to him was people were fighting, he orchestrated all of it, and now he could tell or show others he was the victim in his own household.

Reflections

CHAPTER 13:

~

Physical Abuse

I need to be clear here. Not every abuser is physically violent, but that does not make the damage any less hurtful or easier to move past. Many of us are confused about what violence is, so I will leave you with this: if he has ever yelled, thrown something, slammed a door, called you a degrading name, entered your physical space to intimidate you, grabbed you, strangled you, thrown you, pushed you, or barricaded you – he has been violent.

Like most, if not all of you, who have experienced physical violence in a relationship, I remember the first time Richard hit me as if it was yesterday. Again, I am sure, like many of you, I did not realize there were so many acts of violence leading up to this day that I was not aware were warning signs.

We were nearly ten years into our relationship. I thought that if a man abused his wife or girlfriend, it would happen much earlier in the relationship as it has for so many women. I believed it would look how it does in the media; one day, you are a happy couple and the next, you have a black eye. In my case, I felt more confused than anything.

I did not realize I was already being abused. Richard was verbally aggressive, physically threatening, and then love-bombing the shit out of me afterwards. But Richard hadn't struck me, and this was my deal-breaker. So I thought.

I look back now and realize how this was all presented so clearly. I had been resistant to commitment for so many years which made me feel like I was in control, but I wasn't. I shared a house with an abuser, three children at the time, and I had been coerced into an engagement. After years of telling Richard that I did not ever plan on being married, he proposed. On my birthday, no less, and the kids were involved and excited. I felt like I could not say no.

The destination wedding was planned, we had several guests who had paid for their trip, and I felt excited and simultaneously trapped by it all. Or, really, I was trapped by my fear of disappointing people. And he knew this. Richard now had me exactly where he needed me to be – in a legally binding union that he hoped I would be unable to walk away from.

That's when Richard chose to up the ante and show me how much power he really had over our household. This occurred before we were married. It was a night when we had all been celebrating our niece's birthday with family. Richard had been drinking. He was intimidating me with looks and his body language later in the night because I wanted to leave, the kids were asleep on the floor and I had been trying to get his attention. I was preparing myself for a regular heated and chaotic one-sided argument when we got home, but it turned out much worse than I had anticipated.

The minute we arrived home and walked through our front door, he ushered the kids to their bedrooms. As I put our daughter on the bed, he approached me and threw me across the room. He was in a rage. The ease at which he was able to throw me into the wall while my daughter sat screaming on our bed was terrifying. He could have killed me. It was as if a switch went off.

I was no longer able to keep myself safe.

I was no longer able to keep my children safe.

My home was not safe.

And I could never love this man again. In fact, I hated him.

Afterwards, he mocked me for crying, and repeatedly yelled that it was my fault he did this.

For the week following, he gave me the silent treatment as punishment for making him step out of character. Then the love-bombing began. I was bombarded with gifts, jokes, spending, him wanting to plan the wedding and constantly inviting people over so I would have to interact with him and pretend to be happy.

Months passed, and I began to wonder if this was a one-time altercation. Maybe Richard would never hit me again. Maybe he learned his lesson, was scared, maybe he was even sorry.

It was not a one-time altercation. But before Richard ever hit me again, I knew I had to go. I was constantly walking on eggshells. I was not sleeping, I was not eating, and I was afraid of him. The second Richard raised his voice; my body would go into panic mode. I could feel my adrenaline increase. I could not think straight, and I'd become so tense I'd instantly get a headache. I began to involuntarily flinch when he was angry or would make a sudden move. If he questioned me about my day, I would feel my throat close, so I couldn't speak. I felt like everything was an interrogation and that nothing I said would be good enough.

The stress of living in this environment left me feeling vacant. I felt like I didn't know myself anymore and that my ability to be emotionally available for myself or my children was diminishing.

What made this worse was that Richard became increasingly more violent in front of his male family members. The less they reacted or intervened, the more powerful he felt, and the more powerless I felt. This would continue to be the theme long after leaving him – with the courts, the police, Children's Aid, lawyers, social workers, and his family.

Here's the deal with domestic violence. It does not just end. Narcissists become more violent to assert their control over you. They rely on those long-time lapses in between altercations to groom you into thinking they won't do it again or you somehow deserved it.

Those who know, know. It takes a split second to go from arguing to bleeding, from addressing a concern to a bruised throat, from crying to broken ribs. If nothing else, I know how fast and easily a woman can be killed by her partner *by accident.*

All it takes is one more time.

This is why I had to leave, and this is why *you* have to go. There are no prayers, hopes, dreams, manifestations, meditations, books or pleading that will stop a narcissist from hurting you. It took me eight years from the first time he hit me to leave. I was terrified. I lived with an autoimmune disease that left me in chronic pain and unsure about my ability to support my children. My children had been deeply affected, and I knew we deserved a better life than this. I did not know how it was going to end, but I refused to die at the hands of a man.

No matter how many times he says he is remorseful, he is not sorry enough to stop. No matter how many times he says he will get help, there is no help for him that includes you. He will make you feel guilty about breaking up his family, which only shows you how easily he can blame you for his choices.

On average, it takes a survivor of domestic violence to leave seven times before leaving for good. If you have departed and returned, you are not alone in this. There is never going to be a right time. The right time is always now.

Reflections

CHAPTER 14:

~

Rewriting History

Rewriting history is a form of gaslighting. The purpose is to convincingly repeat the narcissists' version of an event until you believe it happened the way they say it did. It's like they are telling you the sky is brown when it's actually blue, but they say it in so many ways that you begin to believe the sky was brown, even for that one day.

The trouble is they believe their own lies so much that their new version of the story sounds believable. You will be left confused, and may even think their version holds some truth. I assure you, they are lying to make themselves the victim or the victor of every story. They can rewrite history, so they come out the hero, triumphant, and even selfless.

If you are ever able to uncover the truth, and I am not suggesting you try, but if you ever come across the facts, you will realize they were always lying about their role in the story. They are constantly exaggerating their heroism at the expense of someone else. The manipulation never ends with a narcissist.

I didn't know what I was experiencing when Richard was re-writing history. Imagine spending eighteen years with someone and not knowing what was happening until several years later? It took me twenty-one years to figure out what Richard was doing. This is why I am sharing this with you. I want you to be armed with the knowledge of what is really transpiring in your relationship.

It's exactly what it sounds like. Something happens where Richard is the perpetrator, then he says something else happened, but in his altered version of the story, he is not the bad person – I was.

I could end this right here, but let me leave you with some specifics.

They genuinely think the events unfolded the way they say they did. This is why you cannot convince them otherwise. So please stop wasting your energy on this. If the narcissist says the sky is purple and the oceans are orange, then so be it.

This, like all the other red flags, began so subtly. Richard would verbally recount events that had taken place, but there would be a few key details changed to make it sound like I had done something wrong or that he hadn't done or said what he did.

Here is an example. My son disclosed that his father had been violent towards him. I called the police. My son told them precisely what he told me, and then they decided to call Richard to ask him his version of the incident. Richard, in his best professional victim voice, told the police that our son was mistaken. He stated our son was in trouble for something that happened at school, and this was his way of not wanting to face the consequences while at his father's home. Richard also told them that our son would sometimes lie because of the circumstances around our pending divorce, and this is what kids do when they seek attention.

With an existing final access order from the courts, the police felt it would be best for my son to return to his father's home. When his father picked him up, he leaned over to him and said, "You know I would never hurt you, and I certainly don't hit you. But, this isn't your fault. Your mother is just very angry with me, and unfortunately, she takes it out on me through you."

So, Richard is abusive. My son tells me, I tell the police and they are of zero assistance. The police tell Richard, and he rewrites history by telling our son the incident did not even occur. They go home. Richard proceeds to call family members to tell them his own version of what had transpired, blaming me, and loud enough that our son hears this recreated version of the story several times before he goes to bed.

This causes the victim to reconsider what they thought they saw or experienced. This is rewriting history. If my son had not recounted the story, and I had not reassured him that I believed what happened in his father's home, he may have actually begun to wonder if maybe he was mistaken. This happened so often in our home over the years that I'm sure the children have recreated their memories of violent events where Richard was not the abuser, or that the abuse didn't take place.

Rewriting history is used to completely change the memory of an event for those who were involved or witnessed it.

Reflections

CHAPTER 15:

~

Discard

The discard is considered the final stage in the cycle of narcissistic abuse. This does not mean the abuse is over. It does not mean the relationship is over. It means that the narcissist has thrown you away like a piece of trash, hoping that you will return even more desperate for their attention. The more desperate you are for their attention, the more compliant or agreeable you will be.

Being discarded can look like many situations, depending on what works best for the abuser to control and manipulate you. It is their final way to show you how invaluable you are to them.

Richard knew if he broke up with me, it would be unlikely that I would return. His discarding was more along the lines of telling me he could do better, he would be better off without me, or by ignoring me for weeks at a time.

Typical of a narcissist, he attempted to move onto another relationship as quickly as possible after I left the relationship. This is also considered a form of discarding. The purpose was not only to prove to our community that *he* was not the problem, but to show me how fast he could move on because I was that invaluable – and *he* was that important to someone else.

In other cases, being discarded is constantly being on the verge of a breakup. It's a cycle of cheating. It is breaking up with you, then returning and hoovering/love-bombing you just for the satisfaction of knowing they can. It is moving on to other relationships quickly – that have likely been groomed for some time before your breakup.

In any case, being discarded will make you feel low, unworthy, and sometimes jealous. This form of manipulation can even make you feel proud when they choose you again over someone else.

Being discarded can have devastating consequences. I have spoken with women who considered ending their lives after years of being discarded and chosen, only to be discarded again. This is a game that keeps abusers excited and feeling as if they are in control of you; along with all of the other women they have wrapped in this cycle.

A discard is most likely to happen when either of you is about to celebrate a birthday or special occasion, when a loved one has passed, or when they feel like the relationship hasn't had enough drama lately.

A discard is also most common when:

You begin to question their lies.

When they feel like you may have found out about their cheating.

If you have recently begun to set some boundaries.

If you have called them out on abusive behaviours or patterns.

When they feel like they are not getting away with as many manipulation tactics as they would like.

They have drained you completely dry of love, money, attention, and resources.

To visualize a narcissist is much like looking at a puppet master. One whose puppets were once pretty and shiny but have been tossed in a dirty garbage can with strings all tangled into one another. When he is bored, he grabs any one of them with no real preference. Whichever one is on top and ready to do whatever he decides to orchestrate.

When he is done with that puppet, he dismissively flings it back into the garbage.

Reflections

Conclusion

❧

Leaving my ex-husband was the most terrifying thing I have ever done. I had no one I thought I could talk to because I was under the impression no one would believe me. Nobody in my family knew what was happening. I had made so many excuses for his behaviour over the years, I was embarrassed to tell people that I did not have the courage or resources to leave earlier. I was worried about my children and that maybe I was making the wrong decision. But there I was, after all those years of manipulation, fear, violence, and what I thought was love. I simply did not know anything different.

I write this hoping you do not make the same mistakes I did because I made many. Some were financially devastating, others morally. And some I feel had continued to jeopardize the safety of my children.

I left one time, and that one time was enough to make me never want to go back. Please plan carefully, and know that everything a narcissist says or does after that point will only be for you to return so they can continue to abuse you.

Narcissists are incapable of love. They want the control they have over you, and they are willing to go right back to the idealization and love-bombing stages to remind you of *how good things can be.*

They do not love you.

They do not love your children.

They do not need you.

They do not value or respect you.

They will hurt you again.

He may kill you.

They may kill themself.

These are the hard truths you must continue to remind yourself of when planning to leave, and the guilt sets in. Nothing will ever be different until you leave.

I have included a safety plan at the end of this book. I highly suggest you use it, even if you do not think your partner will become violent. This could be the first time and the last time if they do.

A high percentage of women murdered by their partners are killed between the time they knows you are leaving and the time you settle into your new place. Even if they have never laid a hand on you before.

An important rule to remember is violence is not only when he physically hurts you. If they have attempted to intimidate you, they have been violent.

Your safety and that of your children are the first of your priorities. Everything else laid out in this plan will reflect this and allow you to remain organized and supported during the process so you do not feel like you can't do this.

Not all people who are charismatic and charming are narcissists, but all narcissists are charismatic and charming. This reminder has been very useful for me, as I live for men who can fill up a room with their presence. These are also the men who seek and attempt to destroy women like us.

I mentioned that I found myself with another narcissist years after leaving my husband. It was the first man I had allowed into my life with the premise of the possibility of a relationship. I thought I had done the work. I thought I was on the right track, and I thought I had built a wall around me so strong and tall; that there was no way another abuser was getting past my internal security.

Then one day, I unexpectedly found out he had a girlfriend of many years. As soon as I confronted him, I knew every word out of his mouth was a lie. He used all of the classic lines to try and back his way out of his mess.

I don't know what you're talking about.

Ohhh her? That's my crazy ex.

You know I'd never do anything to hurt you.

I've never known anyone like you.

Please, let's meet so we can talk.

It was at that moment, I knew I was dealing with a liar. However, it was not until I had several amicable and honest conversations with his girlfriend(s) that I realized how much of a liar and a coward he was. From that moment on, I could tell you exactly what he was going to say, how he would say it, and when he would say it.

Plus, it didn't stop there. Conversations with mutual acquaintances allowed me to understand that this was who he was. He lived his life lying to women, taking money, using them, and crying victim when confronted. He was a classic narcissist. The main difference between my ex-husband and him?

He was not violent – with me anyway.

My point? Even after several years of working on myself, I had still fallen for the idealization stage. However, I had the privilege of consulting with my therapist, and it dramatically changed my sessions' direction. My narc-radar is now fully functioning – I think.

Living with abuse is debilitating at the best of times. Over time, it changes how we view the world not only through our eyes but also with how safe we feel in our own bodies. Changes have happened to your nervous system. Your ability to feel safe has been taken away from you, and you may feel unable to make small decisions because of enormous self-doubt.

However, leaving, as terrifying as it is, will be the only way you can begin to heal. You cannot heal going back to the person who hurt you. They will never change, you will never get closure, and you may not get what you need through the judicial system. You have to be flexible and kind enough to yourself to get through it all. When you cannot find the strength in yourself to keep moving forward, you must reach out and ask for help from someone you are close to or an organization committed to helping you.

There are so many things to consider when you move on. Safety is number one, always. Educating yourself on narcissistic abuse is a huge step towards healing. Knowing how to recognize the signs is not enough, though. Next, you will have to do the work to learn how to establish boundaries that narcissists cannot get past and how to prohibit yourself from seeking out what is comfortable and familiar for you.

I have realized that what is healthy is actually very uncomfortable for me. If my nervous system is not activated by mild chaos, a little drama and feeling needed and worshipped, then I'm bored. However, the truth is, I am not actually bored; I just do not know how to be comfortable when my nervous system isn't being activated.

Trust me, therapy has been both eye opening, educational, exhausting, and dedicated work. When/if seeking support in healing, I advise you to keep in mind you may need to interview several people or groups before finding one that is right for you. Please do not waste your time with someone who you are not connecting with. It's not a one size fits all situation.

Secondly, if you do choose to go this route, ensure your therapist or healer specializes in Narcissistic Personality Disorder, Domestic Violence, and Complex PTSD. If you are committed to a therapist, ensure it is one who works with more than one modality so your unique and individual needs can be met.

Moving forward, my only wish is for you to be safe. I want you to have an opportunity to move on and find love in any capacity you choose. For this to happen, you will have to learn to forgive yourself.

Forgiveness has been a huge challenge for me. I had to learn to forgive myself for not speaking up when I should have, for being afraid to contact the authorities, ignoring the signs, for being too scared to leave, for not keeping my children safe, and most of all, for walking away from myself.

The guilt will keep you from moving on, but this is one choice that must be made.

Forgiveness for the narcissist is an entirely other discussion. I think expecting a victim of abuse to forgive their abuser is abusive in itself. If you choose to forgive them, go for it, and if not, all the power to you.

And, if you find yourself with another narcissist, forgive yourself for that one too.

Reflections

Safety Plan

~

A lthough many women have left their abusers, only some have lived to talk about it while others have not. If you have an opportunity to plan, you should leave with your eyes wide open.

**If you need to leave without a plan for safety reasons, contact a local women's shelter and follow their direction. *This* is what they are trained to help you do.

The following is a list of things you should consider before you leave (in no particular order):

1. Consult a lawyer first. If you cannot pay for legal representation, most courts will have a duty counsel on staff for family court issues. If you can pay a lawyer, I would highly suggest hiring a lawyer who is familiar with domestic violence cases. If they are not, there is a chance they will persuade you to stay or will make you doubt your choices. The general public does not understand narcissistic abuse.

2. Tell someone you can trust that you are planning on leaving. Make sure their phone number is on speed dial, and they know your plan to the minute. They should have clear instructions on what to do or who to contact if they

cannot reach you. If there is an emergency, there should be someone waiting to hear from you. Instruct them to notify a shelter or the authorities if they do not.

3. Notify your local police department and tell them your plan, particularly if there is a history of violence. The police do not offer the same support to every person according to race, mental wellness, ethnicity, or language – this is a fact. Ensure the person supporting you understands what your fears or expectations are of the police and plan around this as well. If it comes down to you or your violent partner in a life or death situation – *you* need to be kept safe.

4. Have someone come to help you move, and make sure they know there is a potential for violence. Give that person clear instructions of what to do if your significant other becomes violent.

5. If you can plan to leave without telling the abuser, do so. Leave while they are not home if this is an option for you.

6. Photocopy all of your government-issued ID, and leave it in a safe place outside your home. It is common for abusers to take your ID and that of the children to make moving forward difficult for you. Take the originals when you leave as well if they are still available to you.

7. If you have had time to plan, open a bank account and leave no trace of it in your home. Put as much money as

you can into it. This may mean as little as $10/wk or as much as thousands. Either way, not having access to your money will seriously halt your ability to move forward.

8. Make copies of your house and car keys and keep them in a safe place. It is common for an abusive partner to try to stop you from leaving by hiding keys.

9. Do not leave any traces of your plan in writing in your home. If he finds it, and you are blindsided by his rage, your safety could be compromised.

10. Reach out to a local shelter for victims of domestic violence to discuss what your options are. You may not need to use them, but you will be glad you have connected with someone there if you do. *This* work is what they do. They will likely complete a risk assessment, which is an important piece of safety planning.

11. Tell people. You will need all the support you can get. Surround yourself with people who will lift you up, be on your side, inspire you, and lend you strength when you feel like you can't do anything anymore.

There will be people who you think will have your back that won't, and there will be people you weren't aware that would, who will. Be okay with all of this. Know there are people who will support you, and these are the people who matter.

Reflections

Resources

~

There are websites where you can learn more about keeping yourself safe, how to efficiently and safely plan to leave and what tools you'll need when and if you contact emergency services. These websites have an emergency exit feature that deletes the history of your current search. This feature was included so you can quickly exit the page if your abuser enters the room. He will not be able to see it if he searches the history.

In Toronto:

www.schliferclinic.com: Barbra Schlifer Clinic offers free legal advice, counselling services, groups, and information.

www.awhl.org: The Assaulted Women's Helpline offers free 24hr crisis counselling, emotional support, information and referrals via telephone to women in up to 154 languages.

Call #SAFE from your Bell, Rogers, Fido, or Telus mobile phone.

Toll Free 1-866-863-0511

Toll Free TTY 1-866-863-7868

GTA 416-863-0511

GTA TTY 416-364-8762

Senior Safety Line: 1-866-299-1011

211toronto.ca can provide safe access to services in your area.

In Canada:

endingviolencecanada.org provides lists and links to support in your city.

END

About the Author:

~

Mirlo Liendo is an author, senior social service professional and survivor of narcissistic abuse. Over the past couple of decades, she has provided counselling to thousands of women and girls experiencing abusive domestic situations, helping them to reclaim their mental wellness, navigate the justice system, access stable housing and cultivate internal courage.

Mirlo is a highly sought after advocate, she has authored articles for publications such as Spacing magazine, been interviewed by Metro Morning, contributed to podcasts detailing narcissistic abuse and intimate partner violence, was profiled in the Tyee series, participated in a Toronto Waterfront Panel focused on precarious housing and was part of an emergency COVID-19 design team that transformed a daycare in a low-income community.

Her debut book, Finding Courage in the Conflict emerged from these experiences.

CPSIA information can be obtained
at www.ICGtesting.com
Printed in the USA
BVHW062112310821
615694BV00015B/1108

9 781777 796211